African Safari

Some of the world's best-known animals live in Africa. Let's go on safari and find out more about everything from lions to meerkats and hippos to ostriches!

Ostriches can run as fast as a car driving through town!

Catch me if you can!

Every **zebra** has a unique pattern of stripes.

It's fashion, darling!

African elephants are more than twice as tall as a grown man and can weigh as much as eight small cars!

I-spy, with my Meerkat eye!

Meerkats stand on their back legs to look out for predators, barking loudly if they see one.

Nine hundred and ninety- nine thousand, nine hundred and ninety-nine, **ONE MILLION!**

Every year, **wildebeest** travel north in search of food. It's called the 'Great Migration' because up to a million wildebeest travel in the herd.

Lions live in groups called prides. A male lion's roar is as loud as a jet taking off. It can be heard up to five miles away!

The amount of weight a **dung beetle** can move is equivalent to a man dragging six double decker buses!

BURP! Pardon me!

Hippos are said to be the most dangerous African animal. Their jaws can snap a boat in half in one bite!

Crocodiles lurk, waiting to catch animals by surprise.

Ready? Steady? SNAP!

NORTH

FUN FACTS

Did You Know?
An adult **giraffe** is so tall it could peek in an upstairs window – without needing a ladder!

Weaver birds build huge nests containing up to 100 separate homes.

WOW!

An **ostrich** egg is as big as about 24 hen's eggs.

Forest and Meadow

Day and night, forests and meadows are buzzing with wildlife. Animals use the trees and grasses to build their homes and to find food.

An **owl's** wingspan is about the same as a child's arms held out wide. But they fly almost silently when they hunt at night.

Woodpeckers tap holes in tree trunks with their bills, then use their long, sticky tongues to grab an insect snack.

Can I take your order?

HOME SMELLY SWEET HOME

Foxes use poo and wee to mark their territory. This tells other foxes to '**KEEP OUT**'!

Squirrels can bury up to 25 nuts in an hour. They use memory and sense of smell to find them again.

Rabbits run from predators in a zig-zag pattern, reaching the same speed as a cyclist.

Wood mice gather seeds, nuts and fruit and store them in underground burrows.

I zigged when I should've zagged

Baby deer are called **fawns**. They lie very still in the long grass while their mothers search for food. Their markings help to hide them from predators.

The diet starts tomorrow!

In its lifetime, a **ladybird** eats up to 5,000 tiny insects called aphids.

Bees collect nectar from about two million flowers to make one jar of honey.

In the Mountains

The lower slopes of mountains are often covered in forests. Higher up, it is windy and cold, but some animals still call it home.

A **mountain goat's** rough hooves grip like climbing shoes. They can jump a car length in a single bound, without slipping.

Last one to the top is the loser!

Mountain lions can jump as high as a second storey window in one leap.

Oh great! Antlers again!

Moose live on the lower slopes of mountains. Males shed their enormous antlers, growing a new set every year.

FUN FACTS

Did You Know? A **chinchilla's** hair is 60 times as thick as a human's hair.

The **alpine chough** has been seen near the top of Mount Everest, the tallest mountain in the world!

Rivers and Streams

Many animals live on or close by rushing rivers and bubbling streams. They have to learn to go with the flow - or they'll be washed away!

Diving beetles live in streams, rivers and lakes. Babies are called larvae and are twice as long as their parents!

That's supper sorted!

...there I was. Minding my own business!

Kingfishers dive into the water to catch fish with their long bills.

Dragonflies dart along the river banks, catching insects. They've been around since the time of the dinosaurs!

Oh, I do miss them!

FUN FACTS

Did You Know?
Pelicans have a stretchy throat pouch that holds fish that weigh as much as ten bags of flour!

Adult **crane flies** don't eat much - a bit of nectar is enough to keep them flying!

Desert Survivors

Boiling days and freezing nights, winds whipping up sandstorms and little food or water. You have to be tough to live in the desert...

Sorry! I can't hear you!

Tastes a bit soapy!

A **camel** can go weeks without water. When it finds some, it can drink two thirds of a bath tub in minutes!

Fennec foxes weigh about the same as a bag of sugar, but their ears are more than twice as long as a man's.

During the day, **jerboas** hide away from the desert heat in their burrows.

The **horned viper** is a venomous snake with horns over its eyes. It moves across the sand sideways in loops, so it is sometimes called the 'sidewinder'.

A **vulture** can eat and digest bones.

Funny bone, anyone?

The **addax** is a type of antelope, with big, curling horns that can be as tall as a five-year-old!

On guard!

A **Scorpion** has huge claws and curled tail with a sting that it uses to paralyse prey and also to defend itself.

The Icy Poles

Some creatures live in unbelievably cold places. Arctic animals live around the North Pole. Although there is no land there, the ice is home to many creatures.

Arctic hares are super-speedy. They can run faster than a top athlete, at speeds of up to 40 miles an hour!

Baby **harp seals** are born with beautiful white coats. As they grow, they moult and their coats turn grey, with darker horseshoe shapes in it.

NORTH POLE

Walruses are enormous, with huge tusks that can grow as tall as a four-year-old child.

Don't think he's spotted us!

Polar bears roam across the ice, looking for seals. They are the biggest mammals in the North Pole and can weigh as much as ten humans.

FUN FACTS

The **wood frog** can freeze solid during winter and thaw again in spring!

Brrrrrr-ribbit!

Male narwhals are sometimes called the 'unicorn of the sea' because they have a long, spiral tusk.

At the opposite end of the Earth is Antarctica and the South Pole. Freezing winds blow across the ice, making it feel even colder. But some animals still live there!

The **wandering albatross** spends most of its life in the air. One flew around the world in just 46 days!

On really cold days, **emperor penguins** huddle together so tightly that ten would fit on an armchair.

Budge up!

Warm enough, Your Majesty?

King penguins have four layers of feathers to help them cope with the freezing temperatures.

Target number one.

Killer whales, or orcas, live in groups called pods. They hunt seals and penguins.

SOUTH POLE

Southern elephant seals are enormous. They weigh almost as much as three tractors. They are covered in a thick layer of fat called blubber to keep them warm.

Did You Know? Antarctica has little or no rainfall, which means it is a desert too!

The **Galápagos Penguin** is the only type to live north of the equator.

WOW!

Beneath the Waves

The ocean is home to many animals, from giant whales to sea creatures so tiny you need a microscope to see them...

Giant manta rays have wide, flat bodies. They are up to seven metres wide — that's more than a two-storey house!

WIDE LOAD

The **blue whale** is the largest animal on earth. Their tongues weigh as much as an elephant and their hearts as much as a ca

The **bottlenose dolphin** only rests one half of its brain each time it sleeps.

Blue whales feed on shrimp-like creatures called **krill**, which are about the same length as an adult's finger!

Open wide!

Great white sharks have 300 razor-sharp teeth. They are super-fast swimmers and have amazing senses. They can feel tiny movements of animals, even if they are quite far away.

Flying fish leap out of the water to escape danger, using their stiff fins like wings to glide through the air.

Herring move in huge groups called shoals. The shoal contains hundreds of millions of fish.

Just trying to be different!

Leatherback turtles travel thousands of miles each year. Some have crossed the Pacific Ocean and part way back again!

The biggest **lobster** ever caught was the same size as a seven-year-old child. It was thought to be 100 years old!

That's disgusting!

Starfish push their stomachs out through their mouths and into shellfish to eat them.

FUN FACTS

Did You Know?
Some **sharks** lay eggs in pouches. The empty pouch is called a 'mermaid's purse'.

The **octopus** shoots ink at attackers, then it escapes.

WOW!

Giant squids have eyes bigger than dinner plates!

The World's Weirdest Animals

Whether it's flying at top-speed, or shocking attackers, some animals are full of surprises...

Peregrine falcons are the fastest birds on Earth. Their dives are as fast as a sports car driving at top speed!

Some people say **koala bears** smell like medicine, because they eat eucalyptus leaves - the oil is used in cold remedies, too!

Dr K. Bear, at your service!

Happy Birthday to you!

Male **frigate birds** have a red throat pouch. It blows it up like a balloon to attract a mate.

Anglerfish have a worm-like fishing rod dangling from their heads. When a hungry fish swims near, the anglerfish gobbles it up!

Who are you calling ugly?

The **diving bell spider** spins its very own submarine full of air that it uses to dive underwater.

How shocking!

The shock from an **electric eel** is powerful enough to knock a horse over!

Fooled again!

The **alligator snapping turtle's** mouth has a worm-like tongue to attract fish. When they swim close... SNAP!

Did You Know? **Jawfish** keep their eggs in their mouths until they hatch.

The **blobfish** is one of the weirdest fish. It looks like bags of saggy jelly!

Bombadier beetles blast their enemies with boiling hot poison.

WOW!

The **glasswing butterfly** has wings you can see through.

Amazing Animal Facts

Crab spiders change colour to blend in with flowers. Then they hide and wait for an insect snack.

Opossums 'play dead' when they are attacked, lying still with their eyes glazed and their tongue hanging out, until the danger has passed.

If the **harvestman** is grabbed by the leg, it sheds it and runs away!

The **spitting spider** spits a gluey substance and venom at its prey. Stuck to the spot and paralysed, the insect has no escape!